West Norfolk

In summer, resident wading birds and other wildfowl are a familiar sight on the grazing marshes of East Anglia, but in winter, the wetlands also welcome many migrants. At **Welney** (*right*) swans are a particular feature. Here Whooper swans come from Iceland to over-winter alongside Bewick's swans, which spend the rest of the year in Siberia. A number of nature reserves, including the Welney Wildfowl Trust, have been established where it is possible to observe the ever-changing bird populations without disturbing them.

The East Anglian landscape is characterised by windmills, some of which grind corn and some serve as drainage pumps. **Denver Mill** (*left*), which stands just south of Downham Market, is a fine tower mill dating from 1835. It retains most of its machinery intact and the old granary is now used as a museum with exhibits which relate to the mill. The ancient market town of **King's Lynn** (*below*) was already a harbour at the time of the Domesday Book and by the 14th century it ranked as England's third port. Still an important commercial centre, the town's prosperity is reflected in the elegant Customs House which overlooks the Purfleet. Built in 1683 as a merchant exchange, it originally had open arcades on the ground floor.

Sandringham House (*above*) has long been a favourite private royal residence. Bought by Queen Victoria in 1862, the landscaped grounds contain lakes fringed by a mixture of native and exotic trees and shrubs, and the house and gardens are open to visitors when the Royal Family are not in residence. About six miles north-east of Sandringham, **Bircham Mill** (*left*) is one of the most outstanding of Norfolk's remaining windmills. Built in 1846, it worked until the 1920s and is now fully restored.

Some of the most spectacular earthworks in England surround the ruined Norman castle in the village of **Castle Rising** (*right*) near King's Lynn. Once of great strategic importance, the castle has an impressive keep with fine Norman arches and vaulting. It is surrounded by an immense earth rampart and an outer ditch which is 60 feet deep.

A few miles south-west of Swaffham is **Oxburgh Hall** (*below*), one of Norfolk's finest manor houses. Built in 1482, the Hall is moated and has delightful formal gardens. The great hall was demolished in the 18th century and much of the interior has been modified to reflect the changing tastes of succeeding generations. The superb Tudor Gatehouse, however, remains in its

original form. It is probably the largest 15th century brick-built gatehouse in England, standing 80 feet high. In the 14th and 15th centuries a flourishing sheep and wool trade brought much prosperity to **Swaffham** (*below*). At the heart of the town is the great triangular market place where an elegant Market Cross stands, topped by a figure of Ceres, the goddess of the harvest. It was built in 1783 by Horace Walpole, M.P. and 4th Earl of Orford.

From its position where the ancient Peddars Way crosses the River Nar, Castle Acre was a village of some importance from the earliest times. It was flanked on one side by a Norman castle and on the other by a Cluniac priory. **Castle Acre Priory** (*below*) was founded late in the 11th century, and the glorious west front still stands almost intact.

The ancient village of **Heacham** (*left* and *below*) lies in a pleasant rural situation overlooking The Wash, and is best known as the centre of Norfolk's lavender-growing industry. More than 100 acres is given over to growing varieties of lavender and herbs, and in summer the scent of lavender fills the air as it is picked and distilled to produce perfume and other products. The village itself, set among trees, has a pretty little green surrounded by old cottages and the beautifully proportioned church is built of small flints.

Famous as the east coast resort which faces west across The Wash, **Hunstanton** is divided into two parts. The modern resort of New Hunstanton sprang up after the arrival of the railway in 1862 and has a splendid sandy beach beneath the cliffs. Unusually layered with red and white chalk and carr stone, the cliff ledges provide a nesting site for a wide variety of sea-birds (*right*). On the cliff-top stands a sturdy lighthouse, no longer in use, as well as the remains of St. Edmund's Chapel.

Adjacent to the popular resort of
Hunstanton is the ancient fishing village of
Old Hunstanton (*above*). Among the
mellow, red-roofed cottages and narrow
lanes there is an impressive medieval church
and a moated manor house which dates from
the Tudor period. The sands sweep round
from Hunstanton providing a quiet beach
which is reached from a cliff-top car park or
by a country lane and across the dunes.

Situated between Brancaster and
Holme next the Sea, is the
delightful village of **Thornham**
(*left*). Until Hunstanton developed
as the major port in the area,
Thornham had a flourishing
coastal trade. It is situated on a
natural creek which is still well
used by fishing boats in search of
the crabs, cockles and mussels
which are found in the mud-flats.

Burnham and Brancaster

The quiet little resort of **Brancaster** (*above left*) now lies a mile inland separated from the sea by the dunes, salt marshes and mud-flats which are characteristic of this part of the North Norfolk coast. This is a popular area with fishermen and yachtsmen who gather at nearby Brancaster Staithe on the creek which opens into Brancaster harbour. The silting-up of the River Burn prevented sailing craft from reaching Burnham Overy and lead to the establishment of **Burnham Overy Staithe** (*below*) a mile downstream. Although it was once a busy little port, it is today linked to the sea only by a sandy creek running between saltings. Popular as a sailing centre it is always busy with small boats. A fine restored tower mill (*above right*), now converted into a private house, stands on the edge of the village.

Between Brancaster and Holkham in the far north of the county lies a group of delightful villages known collectively as The Burnhams. **Burnham Market** (*below*) is the largest and most central. This handsome market town has grown up around its market place and its tree-shaded green which is lined with fine buildings including a number of elegant Georgian houses.

One of the more outlying villages, **Burnham Thorpe** (*above*) has a wide green surrounded by brick and flint houses built in Georgian times. The village is closely associated with Lord Nelson who was born here in 1758 when his father was the rector. He was baptised in the tiny 13th century Church of All Saints', and in 1905, the centenary of the Battle of Trafalgar, the church was restored as a memorial to the great admiral. The church contains a marble bust of the man widely regarded as the founder of the modern navy.

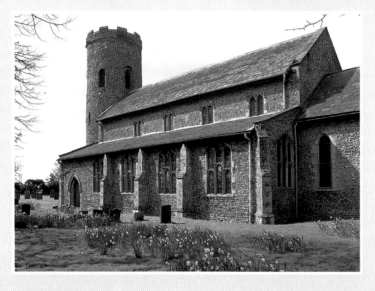

Burnham Norton (*left*) sits in splendid isolation off the coastal road overlooking the salt marshes. Nearby stand the ruins of a Carmelite friary. Founded in 1242, it became a thriving community of about 15 friars but was closed as part of Henry VIII's reformation. The church, which is dedicated to St. Margaret of Antioch, has one of the most complete round towers in Norfolk, built between 1000 and 1066.

Wells-next-the-Sea and Blakeney

Long dependent on the sea for its trade, the delightful town of **Wells-next-the-Sea** is now a mile from open water. Although coasters no longer call at the quay and the fishing fleet is reduced in size, Wells still has a bustling quayside and the harbour (*middle*) continues to provide shelter for fishing boats and pleasure craft. Bustling Staithe Street (*top*) leads down to the quay while small-boat activities are centred at the picturesque East End of Wells. The East End is the older part of the town and here there are many attractive flint-built cottages. The creek provides safe moorings for the numerous small craft which are found exploring the North Norfolk coast and its creeks and inlets. Here, too, the local Sailing Club is based and holds many of its events. A sandy beach, backed by colourful bathing huts (*below*), lies about a mile to the north and can be reached by road or on foot along the sea-wall.

Connecting Little Walsingham with Wells-next-the-Sea, the **Wells and Walsingham Light Railway** (*left*) is a popular attraction. It runs on a section of the old Wells and Fakenham Railway and, at four miles, is believed to be the world's longest 10$\frac{1}{4}$ inch gauge line.

Stretching for twelve miles, the Holkham Nature Reserve (*right*) is the largest coastal reserve in England, comprising unspoiled dunes, beaches and salt-marshes. **Holkham Hall** (*below*) is one of the finest Palladian mansions in the country. It was built between 1734 and 1759 and is known for its superb Marble Hall and Statue Gallery. The house stands in a park landscaped by Capability Brown. There is also a fine walled garden and a stable block which houses a collection of bygone equipment.

The attractive market town of **Fakenham** (*above*) has a number of fine Georgian buildings round the market place. The notable church contains some interesting brasses and colourful Victorian stained glass. The beautiful village of **Little Walsingham** (*right*) boasts many medieval and Georgian buildings, notably those grouped around the 16th century Pump House in Common Place. Little Walsingham has been a place of pilgrimage for nearly 1,000 years and boasts both a 12th century Augustinian priory and a Franciscan friary.

A lane leads down from the little village of **Morston** (*left*), just west of Blakeney, to a tidal creek where The National Trust owns an extensive stretch of the marshes together with Morston Quay. A viewing gallery provides superb vistas along the coast with its teeming bird-life.

Once the foremost port along the North Norfolk coast, **Blakeney** looks out across an expanse of saltings towards the nature reserve at Blakeney Point. Although the estuary has silted up somewhat, the winding creek is still a popular boating centre and there are safe moorings at Blakeney Quay (*above*). The fine tower of St. Nicholas's Church (*right*) is a prominent local landmark and the slender turret on the north-east end of the chancel, which dates from 1220, houses a beacon light which was once an invaluable guide to shipping. There is a superb hammer-beam roof in the nave and much beautiful woodwork throughout the church. Running steeply down to the harbour, the High Street (*bottom*) is lined by attractive houses and cottages, many of which have walls made of local rounded flints.

Boat trips (*right*) can be taken from nearby Morston Quay to Blakeney Point where, in addition to the important bird sanctuary, both grey and common seals can be seen basking on the sand-bars.

In the Middle Ages before the sea retreated, the little village of **Cley-next-the-Sea** (*left*) was a thriving port for the export of wool. The chief landmark in the village is its splendid 18th century windmill which stands on the old quay at the edge of the salt marshes. Dating from the 1820s, it was originally used to grind corn and is a popular subject for artists and photographers. The delightful coastal village of **Salthouse** (*below*) consists of an attractive jumble of stone cottages and possesses an historic hall and manor house. Dominating the village is the church tower which dates from the 13th century, although much of the church was rebuilt later. A long shingle bank has been built up to protect Salthouse from the sea which has invaded the village at least six times during the last century.

Sheringham and Cromer

Midway between Cley and Sheringham is the village of **Weybourne** with its steep shingle beach and deep inshore water. Now it is popular with fishermen, but in the past it has been of some strategic importance. During the First World War troops embarked for France from here and at one time this deep-water port provided such a threat from invading fleets that in 1588 it was garrisoned against the Armada. Picturesque Weybourne Mill (*top left*) stands beside the coast road. A five-storey red brick tower built in 1850, it was converted into a private residence in the 1920's. All Saints' Church (*left*), which is surrounded by the ruins of an Augustinian priory, dates from the 11th century but the handsome porch, of brick-and-flint chequer work, was added some four hundred years later.

Running from Old Sheringham along the coast to Weybourne and inland as far as the delightful Georgian town of Holt, the leisurely **North Norfolk Railway** (*bottom left*) is a preserved steam line. Seen here near Sheringham, it runs for more than five miles through an Area of Outstanding Natural Beauty along a route which was once part of the extensive Midland and Great Northern Joint Railway. Much of the centre of the attractive country town of **Holt** (*bottom right*) was destroyed by fire in the early 18th century and so the architectural style of the town reflects Georgian and later periods. It is perhaps best known for its famous school – Gresham's, founded in 1555 – but the restored medieval church also contains much of interest including a fine window depicting scenes from Chaucer's *Canterbury Tales*.

Until late in the 19th century the resort of **Sheringham** was just a small fishing village. With the arrival of the railway in 1887 it became a popular destination and today it is a pleasant residential and holiday town. Well known for its brightly coloured crab boats, it still retains its quaint fishermen's quarter where fishing boats are drawn up on the beach below the promenade at Fishermen's Slope (*above*).

A mile or so inland at Upper Sheringham is Sheringham Park and Hall, built in 1812 to a design by Humphry Repton. The delightful wooded park (*right*), which is now National Trust property, is particularly known for its rhododendrons and azaleas. The woods at **Pretty Corner** (*below*) on the outskirts of Sheringham provide a popular spot for picnics.

Between Sheringham and Cromer are the twin villages of West and East Runton. Not so many years ago these were simple rural villages but now they are popular little holiday resorts, each with its own sand and shingle beach where crab boats provide a splash of colour when they are drawn up on the sands. The beach at **West Runton** (*above*) is situated in one of the few gaps in the cliffs which occur along this stretch of the coast. Behind the village there is some fine wooded countryside which includes Beacon Hill, at 329 feet the highest point in the county.

The old village of **East Runton** (*left*), preserves its rural character with an attractive green and pond, surrounded by flint cottages. Not far distant stands **Felbrigg Hall** (*above*), a well-preserved Jacobean mansion containing original 18th century furniture and pictures. One of its chief delights is its fine walled garden which originally provided fruit, vegetables and herbs for the household.

With its gently sloping beach of good firm sand, **Overstrand** (*top*) is popular for family holidays. The beach is reached by steps or winding paths down the lofty cliffs and a ramp enables fishing boats to be drawn down to the shore. Originally a small fishing village, **Cromer** (*middle* and *bottom*) has now developed into the principal resort on the North Norfolk coast, known for its fine beaches, cliff scenery and invigorating climate. A massive sea-wall, built to prevent encroachment by the sea, provides access to the beach from the promenade. Alongside the Victorian hotels and boarding houses, the narrow streets of Old Cromer recall the time when the crab-fishing industry flourished. Although the number of boats working out of the town has diminished in recent years, fishermen still launch their boats from the beach to catch the famous Cromer crabs as well as other fish. The old part of the town is clustered around the magnificent Church of St. Peter and St. Paul. With its 160 feet high tower, the tallest church tower in Norfolk, it occupies a commanding position in the centre of the town.

Poppyland

When the railway reached North Norfolk in the latter part of the 19th century, this coast with its clear light, invigorating air and unsophisticated charm had great attraction for romantic Victorian visitors. Entranced by the sight of all the wild poppies growing in cornfields and on cliff-tops, they coined the name **Poppyland** (*below*) for this newly discovered area. The title came to be associated particularly with the area around Cromer. Standing beside the road from Mundesley to Paston is **Stow Mill** (*left*), a fine black-painted tower mill complete with sails and restored cap and fanwheel. It was built in 1827 and last worked in the early 1900s when it was converted into a dwelling.

Situated on a low cliff-top amidst cornfields and country lanes **Mundesley** (*right*) is a small resort combining the pleasures of both coast and country. The wide sandy beach, backed by a small promenade, provides good bathing, and boats can be launched from the sands. The poet William Cowper stayed at Mundesley on more than one occasion and the fine Georgian house where he stayed can still be seen in the High Street.

South of Cromer the coastline is studded with little coastal resorts, each with its own character and charm. **Bacton-on-Sea** (*above*) extends along the coast road, its wide sands protected by groynes and a sloping sea-wall. A cliff-walk which offers fine sea views links Bacton to Walcott and **Walcott Gap** (*right*) where steps lead down to the sands. Since 1791 the distinctive red-and-white banded lighthouse at **Happisburgh** (*below*) has warned shipping away from a treacherous sandbank which runs parallel to the coast for about nine miles.

Severely damaged by a fire in 1600, **North Walsham** (*left*) was largely rebuilt in Georgian times, a fact which is reflected in many of the handsome buildings which surround the Market Place. The unusual market cross with its triple dome was originally built in the mid-16th century and restored in 1897 to mark Queen Victoria's diamond jubilee. In the Middle Ages **Worstead** (*below*) became a centre for the wool trade and the technique introduced by Flemish weavers produced a cloth which became known as worsted, after the village. The impressive church is a legacy of the prosperity brought by the weaving trade.

One of the most outstanding of Norfolk's great houses, **Blickling Hall** (*below*) near Aylsham was built between 1619 and 1627. With its Dutch gables, turrets and clock tower, it is known for its superb long gallery which houses one of the finest libraries in the country containing many early printed volumes. The house stands in beautiful wooded parkland and has some superb Jacobean-style gardens. The grounds include an attractive crescent-shaped lake, an orangery and a temple.

Broadland Coast

A wide, sandy beach studded with rock pools is separated from the village of **Sea Palling** (*left*) by dunes planted with marram grass to hold up the process of erosion. From the village there are pleasant walks through designated Areas of Outstanding Natural Beauty. At **Horsey** (*below*) the dyke and mere are popular with small-boat enthusiasts. Horsey Windpump was originally built to help drain the marshes by pumping water from the dykes into the river. This fine tower mill continued to work until 1943 when it was severely damaged by lightning. It has now been restored and is one of the largest mills remaining on the Broads.

The attractive village of **West Somerton** (*right*) is known as the home of Robert Hales, the "Norfolk Giant". Born in the village in 1820, he grew to a height of 7 feet 8 inches and is buried in the village churchyard. West Somerton Staithe lies close to the coast road and footpaths lead inland to Martham Broad, sometimes also known as Somerton Broad. This peaceful spot on the River Thurne is an important breeding ground for birds such as the bittern and the harrier.

A short way along the coast from Caister, the little holiday villages of **Scratby** (*above*) and California have superb sandy beaches backed by crumbling cliffs which, like so many places along this coast, are constantly under attack from the elements. Boats are launched directly from the beach in the little fishing village of **Winterton-on-Sea**. Daniel Defoe, author of *Robinson Crusoe*, visited the area in the 1720s and recorded that half the houses in the village were built using timber taken from wrecked ships.

A particular feature of the county is the village sign. Frequently elaborate and highly coloured, these signs are normally prominently sited and depict features or events closely linked with the particular village. **Hemsby** retains its village atmosphere, although it is Norfolk's second largest resort after Great Yarmouth some six miles away. A popular destination for family holidays, Hemsby has a wide, sandy beach (*above*) backed by dunes and offers a variety of entertainments and seaside amusements. The low cliffs which extend from Hemsby along the coast to Caister-on-Sea are constantly subject to erosion, and cliff-top buildings have continuously been in considerable danger of crumbling into the sea.

The attractive little holiday resort of **California** (*above*) took its name from the American state of the same name after a hoard of 16th century gold coins was found at the foot of the cliffs near Scratby in 1848. Houses were built on the cliff-top and, as the Californian gold rush was much in the news at the time, the new hamlet was given the name California.

Scroby Sands is a large sandbank formation sited two miles off the coast near Caister. It is the location of a large-scale offshore wind farm. Officially opened in 2005, it will eventually produce enough power annually to meet the energy demands of more than forty thousand homes.

Caister-on-Sea is a quieter resort than its lively neighbour, Great Yarmouth, although it was an important port in Roman times. It is surrounded by delightful country walks and about a mile from the village stands 15th century Caister Castle, the first brick-built castle in England. It was built in the 1430s by Sir John Fastolf, the model for Falstaff in Shakespeare's Henry IV, on his return from the battle of Agincourt. Although it is now in ruins, the tower, surrounded by a moat, is still an impressive local landmark.

Around Great Yarmouth

An ancient town which dates at least from Norman times, **Great Yarmouth** has for centuries been an important centre of the fishing industry, known especially for its herrings. There is still a busy commercial harbour (*below*) providing safe anchorage for a variety of coastal vessels. With the arrival of the railway in the 19th century, came the tourists and a whole new leisure industry. Great Yarmouth now has two piers, attractive parks and gardens and the large Marina Centre.

The Yacht Station (*above*), situated where the River Bure meets the River Yare, is always busy with leisure craft and there are boat trips along the River Yare and onto the Norfolk Broads. Four miles of sandy beaches offer a variety of traditional seaside entertainments and at night the front becomes a blaze of coloured lights.

Situated opposite Yarmouth on the other side of the River Yare, **Gorleston** (*above*), with its colour-washed houses and disused lighthouse, is a popular resort in its own right. The sandy beach is backed by the upper and lower esplanades which are separated by a wide expanse of grass. The Yachting Pool, located on the beach near the south pier, is a popular attraction. **Burgh Castle** (*left*) is one of a chain of castles built by the Romans to defend the east coast against Saxon invaders. Situated where the River Yare runs into Breydon Water, sections of the massive walls still stand surrounded by a flat expanse of marshland.

Also situated at Burgh Castle is the colourful marina (*right*) which attracts both yachtsmen and holiday-makers. With its pontoon moorings, slipway and boat-building services it provides welcome facilities for small-boat enthusiasts. Visitors also appreciate the riverside pub and the beautiful scenery along the River Waveney.

Norfolk Broads

The network of meandering rivers and open expanses of water which make up the Norfolk Broads creates an environment which is unique throughout Britain. The twelve large and twenty-four small lakes or meres are interlaced with dykes and rivers which provide nearly two hundred miles of navigable waterways. A wide river flowing through open country, the Thurne is an ideal stretch of water for sailing and other boating activities. The smaller River Ant winds between reed marshes which provide a perfect habitat for water-loving birds.

A well-known landmark which was originally built for drainage, **Thurne Mill** (*above*) stands at the entrance to the dyke which leads to the village of Thurne. On the north bank of the River Thurne, **Potter Heigham** (*right*) is a popular touring centre. Hotels, shops and boatyards are all gathered around the medieval bridge where the central arch is so low that many boats have to wait for low tide to pass safely beneath it.

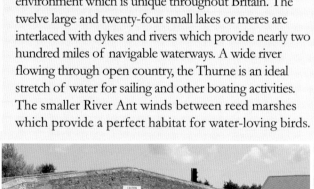

A particular feature of the Broadland landscape is the windmill, although today relatively few survive intact. **Turf Fen Mill** (*left*) is one of Norfolk's many drainage mills which have now largely been replaced by steam and electric pumps. It stands on the edge of Reedham Marsh beside the River Ant. **Wroxham** (*below*) was the first of the Broadland villages to cater for holiday-makers when a boatyard began to hire out yachts towards the end of the 19th century. It is now one of the principal boating centres on the Broads. The fine old bridge, which was built in 1614 and later widened, joins Wroxham with its twin village of Hoveton and offers delightful views of the River Bure as it winds through some of the most appealing countryside in the county.

With its shops and cottages grouped around the green beside the staithe and its three riverside inns, **Horning** (*below*) on the River Bure is one of the most popular ports of call on the Broads. Among the many pleasure craft which sometimes moor here are the sturdy but graceful tall-masted Norfolk wherries which once carried commercial cargoes along the shallow, winding waterways. A short distance downstream is Horning Ferry, an ancient river crossing which has been in use for over 1,000 years.

Norwich

At the time of the Norman conquest, Norwich was one of the largest cities in England. During the Middle Ages it prospered from the lucrative wool trade and became a medieval city of great beauty, surrounded by a four-mile-long city wall. The long and varied history of the city is reflected in its many interesting old buildings and quaint corners.

Beautiful **Norwich Cathedral** (*left*) was built by the Normans who laid the foundation stone in 1096. Considered to be one of the finest ecclesiastical buildings in the country, it is known for its extensive cloisters and its fine array of flying buttresses. The lofty tower with its slender spire rises to 315 feet and, among English cathedrals, is second only to Salisbury in height. The nave roof is decorated with a splendid series of bosses which tell the story of mankind from the Creation to the Last Judgment.

At **Pull's Ferry** (*right*) the ancient gateway to the cathedral takes its name from an 18th century ferryman who plied across the River Wensum. The old ferryman's house stands next to an ancient flint water-gate which, in the 15th century, guarded a little canal through which some of the stone used to build the cathedral was brought at the end of its long journey from Normandy.

In the old quarter of the town picturesque, flint-cobbled **Elm Hill** (*left*) is lined with charming timber-framed and colour-washed houses. Many of them date from Tudor or Georgian times and are preserved much as they would have looked 400 years ago, although today many of them house antique shops and craft centres. The elm tree which gave the street its name stands at the top of the hill.